Gustave Doré · Engravings

GUSTAVE DORÉ ENGRAVINGS

Alpine Fine Arts Collection (UK) Ltd
Publishers of Fine Art Books
London

Editorial coordination and design:
© 1995 by Ninic & Ninic Publishers Ltd. Israel
Published in 1995 by:
Alpine Fine Arts Collection (UK) Ltd.
43 Manchester Street
London W1M 5PE England

ISBN: 0-88168-018-4

Printed in Slovenia by Tiskarna Ljudske Pravice, Ljubljana

Contents

Gustave Doré

Gustave Doré (1832–1883) was an artist of outstanding abilities who was undoubtedly the greatest illustrator of the 19th century and whose influence had a profound effect on the art of his time and as well as the present.

The artist was born in Alsace and grew up in the city of Strasbourg. Doré was a talented artist who was not only a draftsman but was also a skilled lithographer, graphic artist, painter and sculptor. He was a very prolific and productive artist who began to paint at the early age of six when his raw talent attracted the attention of art teachers who saw great promise in the young boy. By the age of thirteen he was already a productive lithographer. He later entered the Lycee Charlemarie in Paris which was to be his only formal art school training. After the Lycee he found work with the publisher Charles Phillipon with whom Doré made an agreement in which he would send one lithograph every week for the next three years for a humouristic newspaper.

Doré from a young age had been interested in classic literature and began illustrating at the age of twelve. At the age of nineteen he experienced much success in illustrating Paul Lacroix's work. Doré then decided it would be his task to illustrate all the worlds most important literature and during this period he changed his medium from lithograph to woodcut. The year 1854 brought about great recognition for Doré due to the publication of Rabelais's humorous novel *Gargantua et Pantagruel* which had been decorated with his illustrations. In 1856 Doré accomplished his first illustrative big book with Sue's *Le Juif Errant* and followed in 1861 with illustrations to Dante's *Inferno* a book that found wide acclaim throughout Europe. Also during that year he illustrated Hyppolit Taine's *Le voyage aux Pyrenees* and Charles Perrault's *Contes*. In the following year for Cervantes novel *Don Quixote* he called upon his own memories about a trip taken to Spain in 1855 with Theophile Gautier and Paul Dalloz. Doré became a very prolific artist and he continued to illustrate several big volumes each year which totalled almost 90 volumes. He also continued to reprint old editions of publications. In 1865 he illustrated Milton's *Paradise Lost*, in 1867 La Fontaine's *Fables* and in 1868 Dante's *Divine Comedy*, in which were produced the illustrations of 'Purgatory' and 'Paradise'. In 1872, nearing the end of his career, he illustrated Blanchaer Jerrold's *The Pilgrimage* in which the imagery portrays exaggerated scenes of man's misery in an industrial country. His last big works were illustrations of Ariosto's epic *Orlando Furioso* in 1872.

One of Doré's most impressive and productive work was *The Illustrated Bible*. The illustrations for The Bible were regarded and still are regarded as Doré's best achievement. In preparation for *The Illustrated Bible* he spent many years researching and studying. He began by looking at the Egyptian and Mesopotanian collections in the Louvre, reading widely on biblical themes and consulting archeological collections from the Near East. During the middle of the nineteenth century many archeological discoveries in Mesopotania took place and the wonders of Babylon and Assyria became accessible to artists like Doré. In many of his biblical scenes Doré depicted Old Testament figures in oriental dress surrounded by exotic draperies which gave great vibrance to the works. In other scenes, such as 'Hell' and 'Purgatory', he managed to combine dramatic atmosphere in a mysterious landscape, whilst in 'David's Victory Over Goliath' the dramatic atmosphere reveals the harsh realities of the scene. Due to their originality and creativity Doré's images for The Bible became a model and inspiration for generations of artists.

The success of *The Illustrated Bible* is apparent in that the first edition sold 3000 copies each month. This continued and ten more editions were subsequently printed. When published in English it spread throughout England, its colonies and America. This was followed by an edition in Hebrew. During the 19th century, this was an almost unprecedented success in terms of publishing and shows how influential Doré's work had become.

As an illustrator his work stood at the forefront of the leading illustrators in Paris at the time and was considered very modern in its manner. He still respected former artistic standards but he moved away from their suggestive influence and searched for his own masterly style and technique in the medium of woodcut. During the 16th century woodcut had become a popular medium, but over the centuries its meaning and illustrative quality had been reduced. But by the middle of the 19th century a revival in woodcut took place and artists began to appreciate its contrasting tones. Doré played a significant role in its revival. Due to his ambitious nature and zealous attitude to work, Doré couldn't cope with such enormous production and thus had to find some associates. He gathered more than forty woodcutters and among them were some of the well known masters like Francois Pannemaker and the painters friend Heliodore Joseph Pisan to whom Doré trusted important scenes. Some of the woodcutters were so skilled that Doré used to make only a rough sketch, leaving them to complete the work. But during the 19th century the technique of the woodcut began to change and became more technical in its production. Thus the mechanical transfer of drawing to the wooden surface also transformed the work which eventually reduced the popularity of the medium.

Like many other illustrators, Doré dreamt of becoming a painter and to express himself through this technique. Although he did produce some successful works of art, he did not manage to adapt the free spirit needed compared to his illustrations. Again, in sculpture he hoped to express his gift of depicting shapes but soon returned to illustrations where his natural flair was evident.

Doré is still considered one of the most significant illustrators of the 19th century. His imagination, expressiveness, special sense of humour and technical brilliance made him an original artist that history has not forgotten.

Rabelais · Gargantua and Pantagruel

The tripes were plentiful, as you will understand,
and so appetizing that everyone licked his fingers.

As soon as he was born he cried out, not like other children:
'Mies! Mies!' but so loud 'Drink! Drink! Drink!'

This discourse concluded, that good man Grandgousier was beside himself with admiration, as he considered the fine sense and marvellous understanding of his son Gargantua.

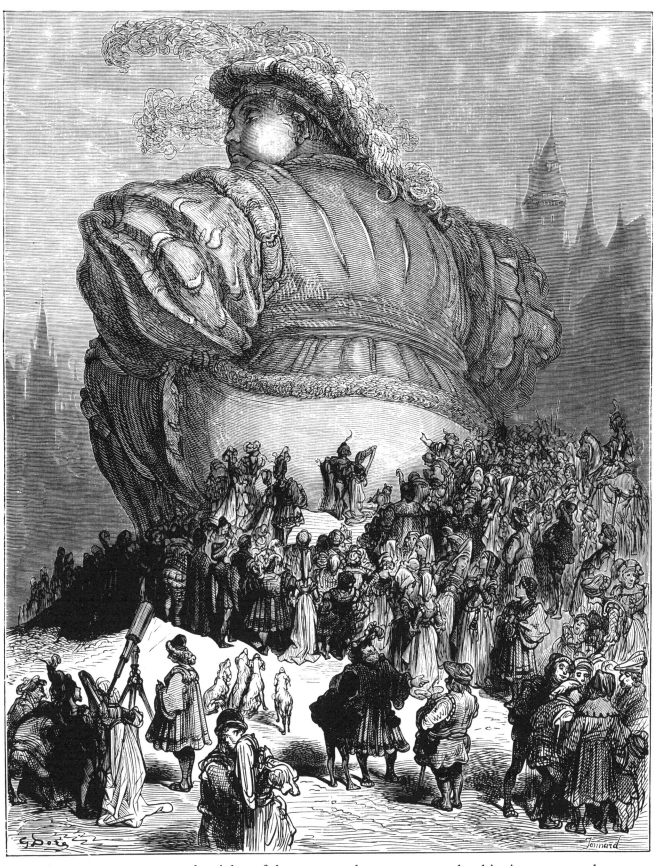

Gargantua went to see the sights of the town, and everyone stared at him in great wonder.

'I think these clodhoppers want me to pay for my kind reception.
They are quite justified, and I am going to give them some wine.'

Meanwhile his servants threw into his mouth, one after another, full bucketfuls of mustard, without stopping. Than he drank a monstrous gulp of white wine to relieve his kidneys.

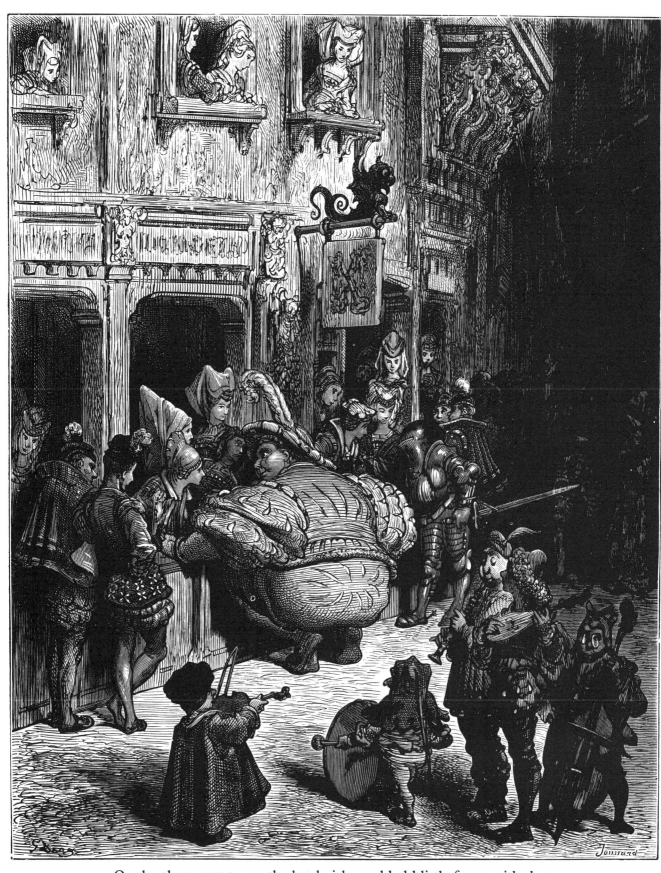

Or else they went to see the local girls, and held little feasts with them,
and collations and postcollations.

So they went on, wasting, pillaging, and stealing till they arrived at Seuilly,
where they robbed men and women alike and took everything they could.

He beat out the brains of some, broke the arms and legs of others, disjointed the neckbones, demolished the kidneys, slit the noses, blackened the eyes, smashed the jaws...

'Oh, if you make me your lieutenant I'll kill a comb for a pedlar.
I bite, I charge, I strike, I seize, I slay, I stop at nothing.'

So he charged with his great tree against it, and threw down the towers and fortifications.
In this way those inside were all crushed and smashed to pieces.

Gargantua and his men came to the mill-bridge and found all the ford so thick with dead bodies...
So here they came to a stop, and considered how they could cross, ...

'Why?' asked Gargantua. 'They're good all this month.'
And pulling at the staff, he picked up the pilgrim with it, making a good meal of him.

So the poor angry wretch went off, and as he crossed the water at Port Huaux, where he related his misfortunes, he was promised by an old witch that his kingdom would be restored to him.

On his departure he graciously thanked all the soldiers of his legions who had been present at this victory, and sent them to winter in their posts and garrisons.

All their life was regulated not by laws, statutes, or rules, but according to their free will and pleasure. They rose from bed when they pleased, and drank, ate, worked, and slept when the fancy seized them.

I will omit to relate here now, at each of his meals,
he swigged off the milk of four thousand six hundred cows.

And so he came to Avignon, and had not been there three days before he was in love.
For the women there love to play the twobacked beast, because it is Papal territory.

When he had performed this feat Pantagruel went to Paris with his party;
and at his entry everyone came out to see him.

30

Panurge's account of the way in which he escaped from the Turks.

But the counsellors, lawyers, and canon-lawyers thought that in so doing he wished also to imply that some kind of human felicity lay in the leprous state, as Our Lord once affirmed.

Then he went to the church where the lady must go to follow the procession, as is the custom on this festival; and when she came in, he gave her the holy water, bowing to her most courteously.

When Pantagruel saw them approaching, he took Werewolf by both his feet,
and raised his body aloft in the air like a pike.

'All the knights of the Round Table were poor starvelings,
who tugged an oar on the Rivers Cocytus, Phlegethon, Styx, . . .'

... Semiramis, a delouser of beggars, ...

After saying this, she retired into her den. But on the doorstep she hitched up her gown, petticoat, and smock to her armpits, and showed them her arse.

Herr Trippa looked him in the face and said: 'You have the physiognomy and metaposcopy of a cuckold, of a notorious and infamous cuckold, I say.'

So you will be to your wife a pattern and example of virtue and goodness,
and you will continually implore the grace of God to protect you both.'

And the whole mob rushed up to see who could get the first date for this precious beating.

The next day nine transports passed us on the starboard side, laden with monks,
Jacobins, Jesuits, Capuchins, Hermits, Augustines, Bernardins, Celestins, . . .

'Magna, gna, gna,' exclaimed Friar John. 'Isn't he a sight, the shitten blubberer?'

In the shady and unfrequented forest, he pointed out several old ruined temples, several obelisks, pyramids, monuments, and ancient tombs, with different inscriptions and epitaphs.

'I believe that all intellectual souls are exempt from the scissors of Atropos,' said Pantagruel.

The crew of the ship *Lantern* towed the spouter ashore on to a neighbouring island, ...

45

The order they kept, their proud gait and their resolute faces convinced us that these were no small fry, but old Chitterling warriors.

The council's decision was that in any event they must stand on their guard.

Into the sow entered these noble cooks, all cheerful, gallant, brisk, and eager for battle.

From a northerly direction there flew towards us a great, huge, gross, grey swine,
with wings as long and broad as the sails of a windmill, . . .

'Very well,' said the devil, 'I shan't fail to be here. In the meantime, do your duty. Work away, peasant, work away! I'm off to tempt the noble nuns of Dryfart to the gentle sin of fornication,...'

The farmer was sad and thoughtful as he returned home,
and when his wife saw his state of mind she thought he had been robbed at the market.

Now note, fellow boozers, that while Greatclod was saying his dry Mass,
three church bell-ringers, each with a great bowl in his hand, were passing among the crowd, ...

As they cleared the first course these maidens sang a melodius epode in praise
of the sacrosanct Decretals.

But Pantagruel insisted that this was the abode of Arete-that is virtue-described by Hesiod, ...

'Send up the master gunner.' The gunner promptly appearing, Pantagruel ordered him
to fire the basilisk, and to be sure and charge it afterwards with fresh powder.

55

Panurge rang, and immediately these smoked birds rushed up, and sang all together. But they had hoarse and unpleasant voices, . . .

'But,' asked Pantagruel, 'once these fine birds have flown away,
do they ever return to the world where they were hatched?'

How with much difficulty we got a sight of the Popinjay.

On the third day after this we came to Sharping Island, the very image of Fontainebleau forest.
For the earth is so thin that its bones-the rocks, that is-stick through its skin.

We passed the Wicket as well, where Pantagruel did not want to land.
And he was right, for we were arrested ...

Clawpuss, from the midst of his Furrycats, addressed us in a furious voice:
'Come on now, come on, come on!'

'...But our queen heals men of every complaint without touching them,
merely by playing them a tune chosen according to the nature of their disease.'

After we had drunk, he took us to see a new convent founded, erected,
and built according to his plans for the Quavering Friars.

Panurge interrogates a Quavering Friar, and only gets monosyllabic answers.

'Most wondrous lady, I beg of you with a contrite heart, let us turn back.
For, by God's truth, I'm dying from sheer fright. . . .'

The marvellous Emblems on the Temple Pavement.

The next picture showed the good Bacchus's attack upon the Indians.

Panurge continued his poetizing as follows:
'Never did the Pythian god / Grant by his divine tripod / Answer surer or more certain. / . . .

Raspe · Baron Munchausen

On looking upwards Baron beheld him hanging by his bridle to the weather-cock of the steeple.

Baron killed fifty brace of ducks.

Baron beheld a noble stag with a fine full grown cherry-tree above ten feet high between his antlers.

Struck fire, and blew up the bear with a terrible explosion.

"For God's sake, sir, your fur cloak is mad!"

Baron made him mount the tea-table.

The Baron's horse drinks in the Market Place.

The Baron helps his horses over the hedge.

A naked man walk upright out of his body.

A second visit to the moon.

As she was passing through a wood, she met Grandpa Wolf.

'You see how it is – we can no longer feed our children.'

When the children realised that they were alone,
they began to call out for their parents and cry with all their might.

83

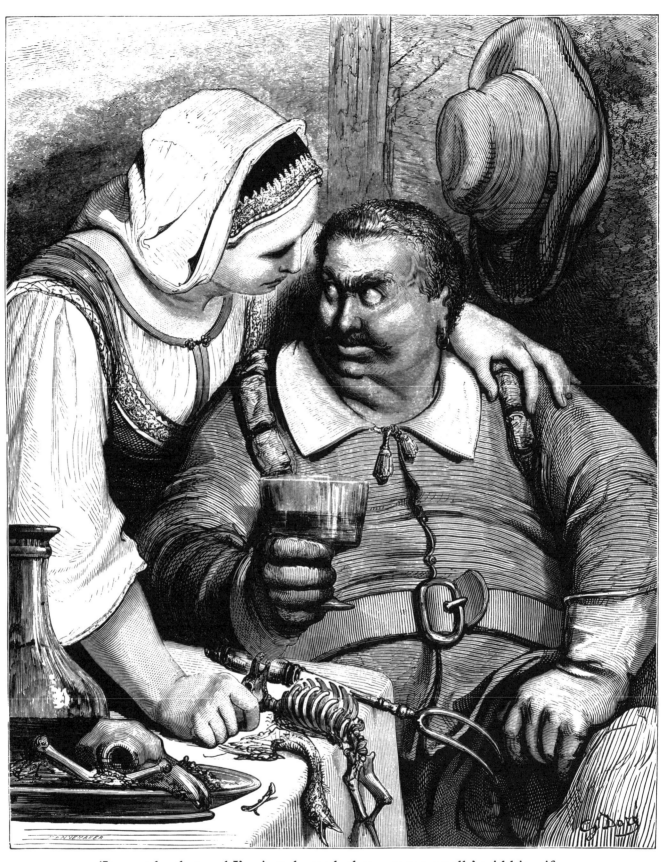

'It must be that veal I've just dressed, that you can smell,' said his wife.

He dragged them one after another from under the bad.

She had never heard a word of the King's orders against spinning with a spindle.

'Help! Help! Monsieur le Marquis de Carabas is drowning here!'

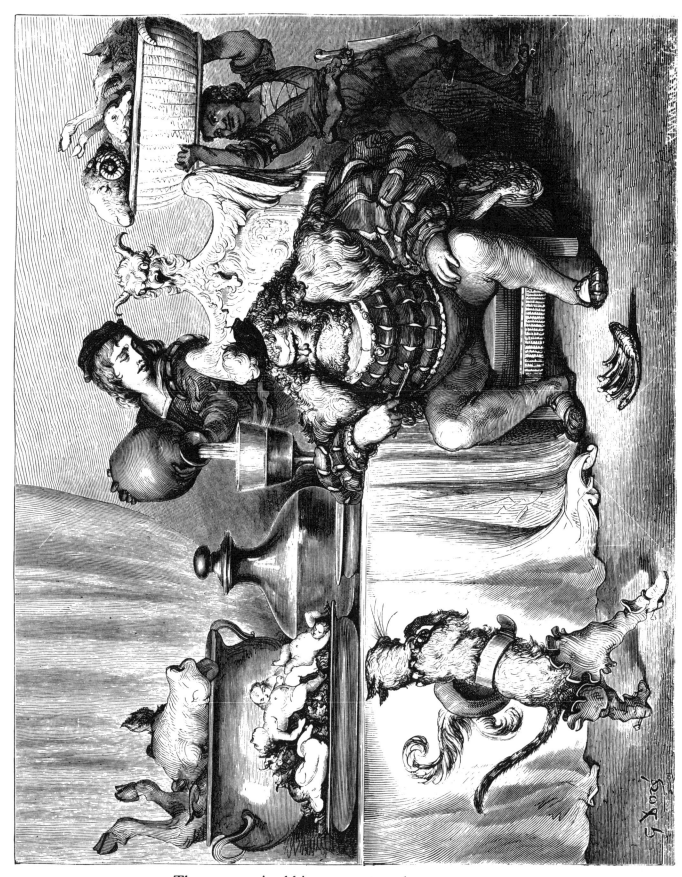

The ogre received him as courteously as an ogre can.

The cat had taken care to find out about this ogre.

One day when she was at the fountain, a poor old woman came up to her and begged a drink.

King's son, seeing how beautiful she was, he asked her what she was doing, there all alone,
and what she had to cry about.

If you do come to open it, there is no saying what I may do in my anger.

The young bride's neighbours and friends,
such was their impatience to see all the riches of her house.

They passed their swords right through his body.

In short, he so buried himself in his books that he spent nights reading
from twilight till daybreak and the days from dawn till dark.

And watched him, sometimes pacing up and down with a peaceful look
and sometimes leaning on his lance and gazing on his armour.

Leading him by the bridle and his ass by the halter, took the road for the village,
much concerned to hear the nonsense that Don Quixote was talking.

Quixote took the same route and struck the same track across
the plain of Montiel as on his first expedition.

At a full gallop and attacked the nearest windmill, thrusting his lance into the sail.

Which invited them, or rather induced them, to spend the sultry hours of midday there.

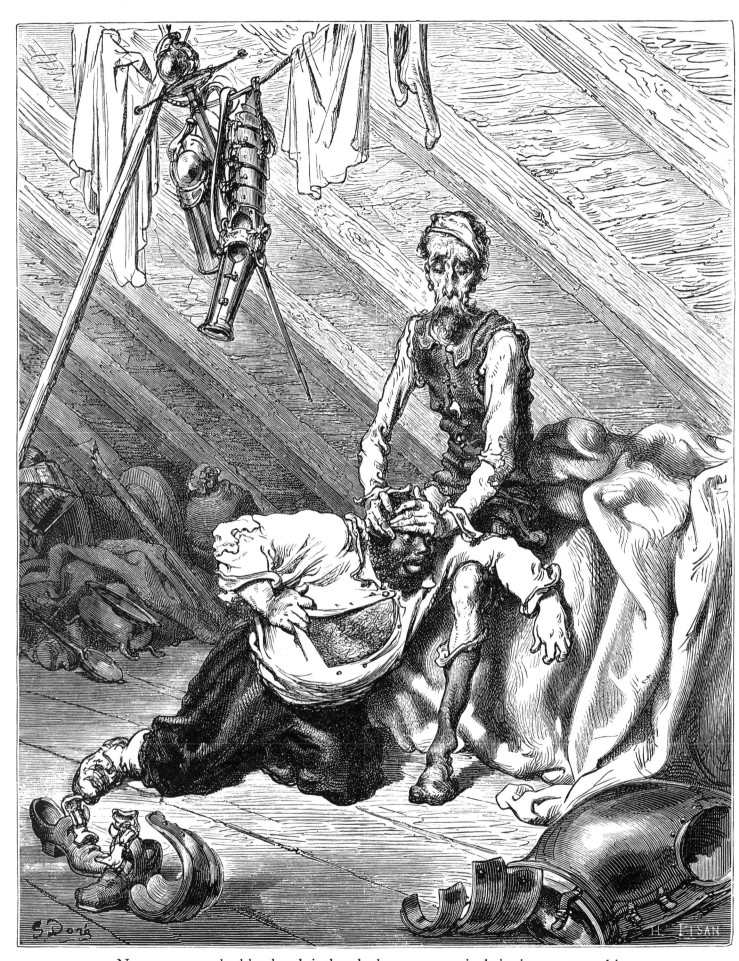

Now no sooner had he drunk it than he began to vomit, bringing up everything that was in his stomach.

But this did not make them stop their tossing and laughter.

And began to spear them with as much courage
and daring as if he were in very truth spearing his mortal enemies.

Now by nightfall they had got into the heart of the Sierra Morena.

He saw on the top of a knoll, which showed up straight ahead,
a man leaping from rock to rock and from bush to bush with extraordinary agility.

'Sir,' replied Sancho, 'is it a good rule of chivalry for us to get lost looking
for a madman in these mountains, where there isn't a road or a track?'

The youth took off his cap; and as he shook his head from side to side,
there began to fall about his shoulders hair which the sun itself might have envied.

108

For he was like a man who finds no difficulty in concluding a bargain because he does not intend to pay.

So it all depends on my master marrying this lady straight away,
sir – I don't know her name yet, so I can't call her by it.

'No more. Cease your praises!' cried Don Quixote at this juncture. 'I hate any kind of flattery.'

Once too when he was posted with a two-handed sword at the approaches of a bridge,
he prevented a whole vast army from crossing.

She stabbed herself, burying the weapon above her breast under her left shoulder.
She then let herself fall to the ground, as if in a faint.

These Arabs cut off his head and took it to the commander of the Turkish fleet.

Then her father came running to us and, seeing his daughter in this condition.

When Don Quixote himself was thus caged and placed on the cart.

Displayed here and now before our eyes, as we might say, a great lake of pitch, boiling hot,
and swimming and writhing about in it a great number of serpents, snakes and lizards.

There the sky seems to him more transparent and the sun to shine with a new brightness.
Before his eyes opens a pleasant grove of green.

Take him to another room where the tables are laid so magnificently that he is speechless with amazement?

'Dawn broke'

'O Tobosan jars, how you bring to my memory the sweet pledge of my great bitterness!'

In the end he awoke drowsy and slothful, and looking all around observed.

122

'What are you grumbling at, Sancho?'

They saw that his eyes were shut, as if in sleep.

I am afraid they will catch them and bring them back tied to their own horse's tail.

Two lackeys or grooms promptly ran out, clothed down to their feet in what they call morning-dress of finest crimson satin, and almost before he had heard or seen them caught Don Quixote in their arms.

I Merlin am who, as the histories say.

Here ended the song of the sore stricken Altisidora.

'Absit!' cried the physician.

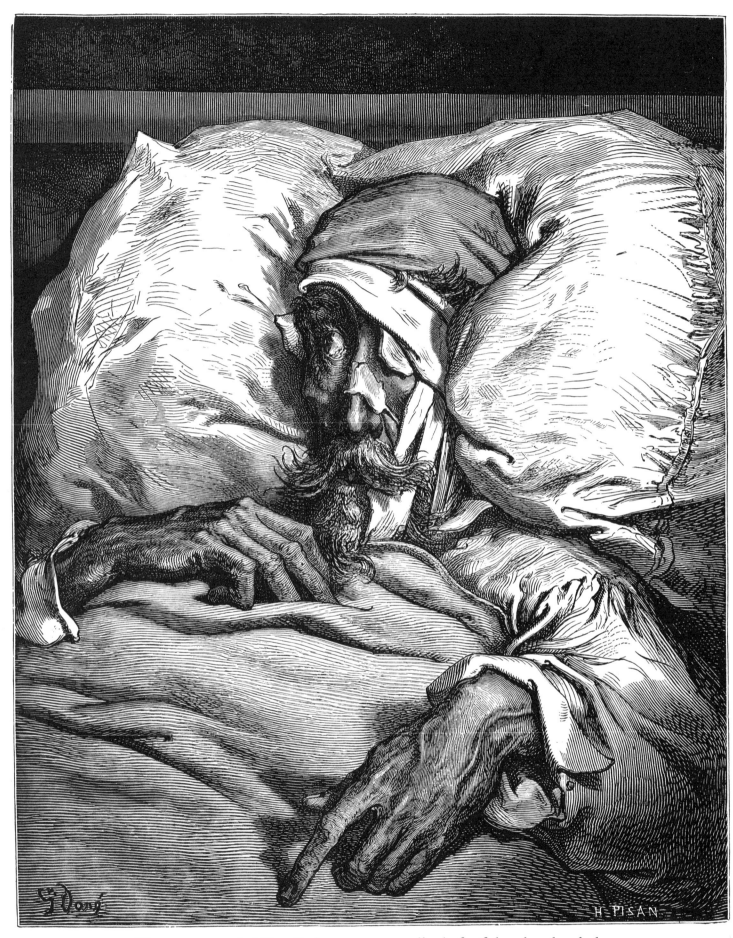

The sore-wounded Don Quixote was exceedingly fretful and melancholy,
with his face bandaged and marked.

He stood up on the bed.

131

'Come here, dear companion and friend of mine, my fellow-partner in my trials and sorrows.'

Making them a speech, to persuade them to give up their style of life,
as perilous for the soul as for the body.

'This life of ours must seem novel to Don Quixote: strange adventures, strange incidents,
and all of them perilous. And I don't wonder if it appears so to him.'

Amidst the same acclamations and music, reached their guide's house,
a large and important one, which proclaimed the wealth of its owner.

However, I stood up to him; I did what I could; I was overthrown.

'On your life, friend, let the matter rest here.'

At last Don Quixote's end came, after he had received all the sacraments and expressed his horror of books of chivalry in strong and moving terms.

And God said, Let there be light.

She shall be called Woman, because she was taken out of Man.

Lord God sent him forth from the garden of Eden.

And Abel, he also brought of the fristlings of his flock and of the fat thereof.

Cain rose up against Abel his brother, and slew him.

144

And the Lord said, I will destroy man whom I have created from the face of the earth.

All in whose nostrils was the breath of life, of all that was in the dry land, died.

And again he sent forth the dove out of the ark.

Cursed be Canaan; A servant of servants shall he be unto his brethren.

Go to, let us build us a city and a tower, whose top may reach unto heaven.

And Abraham lift up his eyes and looked, and, lo, three men stood by him.

Then the Lord rained upon Sodom and upon Gomorrah brimstone.

And Abraham rose up early in the morning, and took bread, and a bottle of water, and gave it unto Hagar.

She said, Let me not see the death of the child.

And Abraham took the wood of the burnt offering, and laid it upon Isaac his son.

And Sarah died in Kirjath-arba; the same is Hebron in the land of Canaan.

Isaac and Rebekah.

And Jacob went near unto Isaac his father; and felt him.

And Jacob dreamed, and behold a ladder set up on the earth, and the top of it reached to heaven.

And Jacob loved Rachel.

And Jacob was left alone; and there wrestled a man with him.

Joseph, being seventeen years old, was feeding the flock with his brethren.

And Pharaoh said unto Joseph, In my dream, behold, I stood upon the bank of the river.

And he said, I am Joseph your brother, whom ye sold into Egypt.

And the daughter of Pharaoh came down to wash herself at the river.

And Moses and Aaron went in unto Pharaoh.

And the Lord called Moses up to the top of the mount Sinai.

The place was called the brook Eshcol, because of the cluster of grapes.

And Moses made a serpent of brass, and put it upon a pole.

And when the ass saw the angel of the Lord, she fell down under Balaam.

169

And Joshua saved Rahab the harlot alive.

170

And all Israel stoned him with stones, and burned them with fire.

And when the men of Ai looked behind them, they saw, and, behold, the smoke of the city.

172

That the Lord cast down great stones from heaven upon them unto Azekah, and they died.

And an angel of the Lord came up from Gilgal to Bochim.

Then sang Deborah and Barak the son of Abinoam on that day.

And Abimelech's young man thrust him through, and he died.

And Jephthah came to Mizpeh, and, behold, his daughter came out to meet him.

And the Spirit of the Lord came mightily upon Samson, and he rent him.

And Samson said, With the jaw of an ass have I slain a thousand men.

Samson loved a woman in the valley of Sorek, whose name was Delilah.

And catch you every man his wife of the daughters of Shiloh.

And David took the head of the Philistine.

So Michal let David down through a window.

So Saul died, and his three sons, and his armourbearer, and all his men.

And ten young men that bare Joab's armour compassed about and smote Absalom, and slew him.

So king Solomon exceeded all the kings of the earth for riches and for wisdom.

Men passed by, and saw the carcase cast in the way, and the lion standing by the carcase.

And Elijah said unto all the people, Come near unto me.

And as Elijah lay and slept under a juniper tree, behold, then an angel touched him.

And there came forth two she bears out of the wood, and tare forty and two children of them.

And Nehemiah viewed the walls of Jerusalem, which were broken down.

So they read in the book in the law of God distinctly.

Then took Haman the apparel and the horse, and arrayed Mordecai.

So the king and Haman came to banquet with Ester the queen.

There came a great wind, and smote the four corners of the house,
and it fell upon the young men, and they are dead.

Now when Job's three friends heard of all this evil that was come upon him.

Isaiah.

The vision of Isaiah the son of Amoz.

198

Then the king of Babylon slew the sons of Zedekiah in Riblah.

Daniel.

Belshazzar the king made a great feast to a thousand of his lords.

And they brought Daniel, and cast him into the den of lions.

Amos.

And Jonah began to enter into the city a day's journey, and he cried, Yet forty days,
and Nineveh shall be overthrown.

There came four chariots out from between two mountains.

And Mary brought forth her firstborn son, and wrapped him in swaddling clothes.

The angel of the Lord appeareth to Joseph in a dream, saying, Arise,
and take the young child and his mother, and flee to Egypt.

In those days came John the Baptist, preaching in the wilderness of Judea.

Then cometh Jesus from Galilee to Jordan unto John, to be baptized of him.

209

Then was Jesus led up of the spirit into the wilderness to be tempted of the devil.

And the third day there was a marriage in Cana of Galilee.

Jesus and the Woman of Samaria.

And Jesus sat down, and taught the people out of the ship.

And Jesus went about all Galilee, teaching in their synagogues, and preaching.

And they brought unto Jesus all sick people.

Sermon on the Mount.

At that time Jesus went on the sabbath day through the corn.

And Jesus' face did shine as the sun, and his raiment was white as the light.

And a certain woman named Martha received Jesus into her house.

There was a certain rich man, which was clothed in purple and fine linen.

And the scribes and Pharisees brought unto Jesus a woman taken in adultery.

And they brought young children to Jesus that he should touch them.

And when Jesus was come into Jerusalem, all princes of the Gentiles exercise dominion over them.

And Jesus went into the temple, and began to cast out them that sold and bought.

Now when the even was come, Jesus sat down with the twelve.

And there appeared an angel unto Jesus from heaven, strengthening him.

Then Pilate therefore took Jesus, and scourged him.

And the soldiers platted a crown of thorns, and put it on Jesus' head.

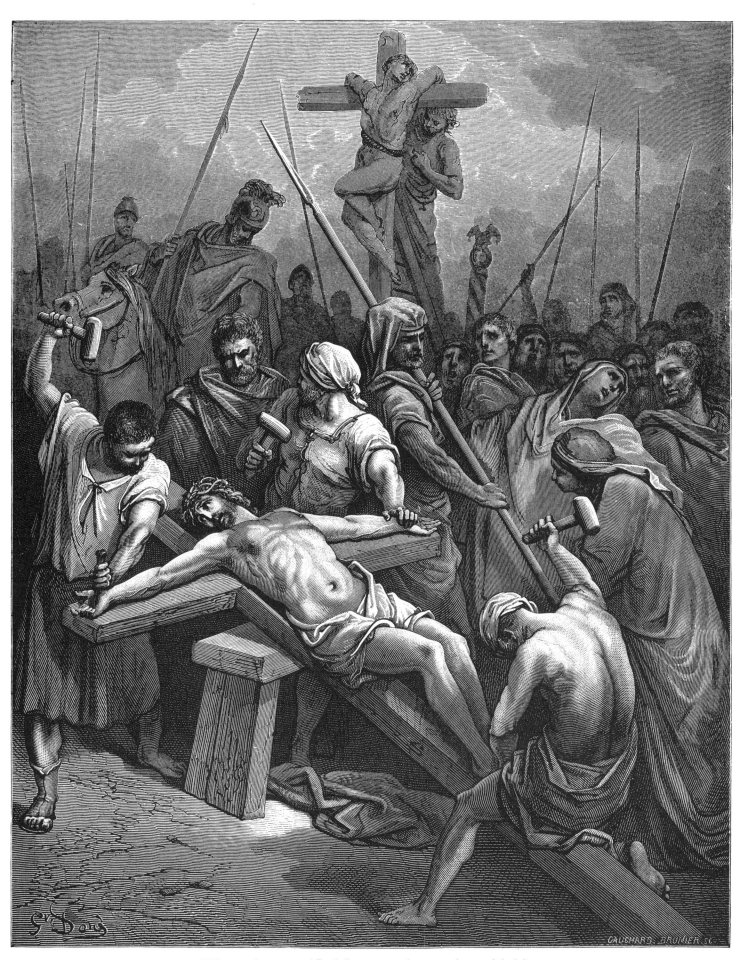

Where they crucified Jesus, and two other with him.

Joseph of Arimathæa, besought Pilate that he might take away the body of Jesus.

While they communed together and reasoned, Jesus himself drew near, and went with them.

This same Jesus, shall so come in like manner as ye have seen him go into heaven.

Saul came near Damascus: and suddenly there shined round about him a light from heaven.

The Revelation of Jesus Christ, sent and signified it by his angel unto his servant John.

A woman clothed with the sun, and the moon under her feet, and upon her head a crown of twelve stars.

And John saw an angel come down from heaven, having the key of the bottomless pit.

And I John saw the holy city, new Jerusalem, coming down from God out of heaven.

The Two Mules.

The Town Rat and the Country Rat.

The Wolf and the Lamb.

The Oak and the Reed.

The Lion and the Gnat.

The Lion and the Rat.

The Hare and the Frogs.

The Miller, His Son and the Donkey.

The Fox and the Grapes.

The Shepherd and the Sea.

The Miser Who Lost His Hoard.

The Little Fish and the Angler.

The Old Woman and the Two Servant-girls.

The Doctors.

The Peasant and the Snake.

The Two Cocks.

The Two Friends.

The Old Man and the Three Youths.